# Getting Your Groove Back

00 01 02 03 04 BIN 10 9 8 7 6 5 4 3 2 1

Library of Congress Cataloging-in-Publication Data
Hall, Amy.
 Getting your groove back / Amy Hall.
  p.   cm.
 ISBN 0-7407-0483-4 (pbk)
 1. Quality of life. 2. Women–Psychology. I. Title.
BF637.C5.H293 2000
158'.082—dc21                          99-40479
                                       CIP

## Attention: Schools and Businesses

Book design by
Holly Camerlinck
Illustrations by
Sharon Watts

# Getting Your *Groove* Back

## The Sassy Woman's Guide to Recharging Your Life

Amy Hall

**Andrews McMeel Publishing**

Kansas City

For Scott, my sanctuary in this world, my champion. For your large heart, loving patience, and "modesty." Thank you for making me laugh so hard through all these years; they've been wonderful.

For Dora Mainwaring, for the big wide world we quietly observed together from the Hancock, and how far we've traveled.

For my father, John, who tenderly told me as I was hyperventilating before my walk down the wedding aisle that I didn't have to do it if I didn't want to.

For my mother, Sue, who clocked me into this world.

For Mary Ann Wells, Sandy Smith, Barbara Winningham, Judy Miller, Tina Kennedy, Emöke Pulay, Myma Jean Miller, and Susan Jennings—special women of my life who've unselfishly loved and nurtured me, taking me under their wings as only good friends and mentors can.

# Contents

# Introduction

To be blunt, the world has a tendency to just plain suck us dry, especially as women. It's a slow process that creeps up on us over the years, through the various phases and trials of our lives. We look up and discover that the bounce is gone from our step, the chronic grin from our faces, the *O* from our orgasms—you get the picture. A sinking feeling starts to set in, that feeling that we are just shells of the women we started out as—we haven't reached our potential, we have become the creatures of habit and discount store shopping we said we'd never be. Where is that spunk and special aura that always set us apart . . . where, oh where, is our Groove? Where did it go?

I do hate to be the hussy that breaks this to you, but guess what? A sense of freshness with the world and with yourself isn't just going to fall out of the sky. As the diva Madonna sang in her hit "Into the Groove," the first directive to getting back a zest for life is to "get up on your feet." You must *work*—you must stand to fight the evil forces of numbness and mediocrity that have taken over your life! You yourself must remove the veil that now shrouds your innate, rejuvenating Grooviness!

Essentially, a joyous balance is achieved when all three of the core areas of life are in shipshape condition:

Our Careers: We must look forward to getting up to go to work in the morning—whatever our *work* may be. What we do must not be just for a paycheck, or else we're all just big prostitutes. Our vocations must give us a sense of pride and success, whether we're lawyers, plumbers, stay-at-home moms, or CEOs.

We must also take care not to be consumed by our careers, despite the constant pressures we face which encourage that terrible condition.

Our Relationships (with romantic liaisons, family, friends): Relationships are wonderful opportunities to grow and learn about ourselves. Also, we simply can't survive alone in the world—we're all codependent in that sense. However, *all* relationships are optional and, more important, *conditional.* Relationships that more often than not depress or anger us steal our Groove. They must be *eliminated* and *avoided,* or *transformed* (but only if it *really* is worth the energy and feasible).

Our Souls: After our jobs and our relations with others are considered, the final component for Groovy contentment is just being happy with who we are. Whatever hell hits the earth, we own and can rely on ourselves. That is a constant in the universe that should give us a

sense of empowerment and pride. To foster
these feelings we must simply nurture ourselves and indulge our whims, getting to
know what makes us tick along the way.

This sassy little book contains the pointers
and reflections you need to get these three
areas of your life back on track and thus
restore your essence, your Groove. The world
has robbed you of it, and it's time to kick
some butt and take it back! Tallyho! Yeah!
Oh baby!

# Getting Your Groove Back

Getting Groove Back in Your

*Career*

This isn't an office.
It's Hell with
fluorescent lighting.

—*Unknown*

I'm a firm believer that if you like your boss, you can be a professional camel dung shoveler and find joy in the workplace. Your direct boss makes the difference. Dream jobs far and wide have turned into nightmares because of managers who are lazy, manipulative, incompetent, self-absorbed, and/or [insert any evil quality imaginable here]. Shop for a good-hearted, intelligent, business-savvy supervisor from whom you can learn. If we apprentice under talented and bright people, our careers will be educational, fun, and fulfilling, no matter what our titles or paychecks. Sharp people teach and groom us, giving us great experience that invariably qualifies us for other jobs in life. Maniacal and inept bosses tire us, cause us not to care about our professions, impel us to call in sick a lot, doubt our abilities, and lose our Groove. Fear them. Run from them. They are evil, bloodsucking vampires clad in tweed who send really stupid E-mails. Run, Run!

*K*now that you will never make the money you are worth, few people do—so don't associate your professional self-esteem with your biweekly contributions to the checking account. The thing that will forever pull our chain as women is that we still consistently earn less than men decades after the Women's Movement kicked off. There are many books out there that teach great salary negotiation techniques for women. Arm yourself with their tips at your next review, and remember that all business transactions in life are negotiable. Do what you can, but don't fret too much in this arena. Money is not the sole purpose of our careers. Anyway, some of my most "financially successful" friends are ready to jump off a bridge because they *hate* their jobs. They want to become basket weavers and own bed and breakfast establishments (in other words, they want to be poor).

Don't be a small lamb led to slaughter, actually believing the complete validity of all memos from those at the top. Sheesh, have a spine—it's pretty fun!

# You're so riled up

you could illegally park in a handicapped space or set a VA hospital on fire. You didn't get the job that you are *so* qualified for, a cool new project got tossed to another department, or whatever. You are mad and, go ahead and admit it, you are paranoid that you have overestimated yourself, that maybe you're *not* all you've hyped yourself to be, you weren't really a "natural candidate," et cetera. Well, humility is good in doses sometimes, but I must share my Susan story to soothe your wounds. There is a real-life Susan who I consider to be one of my best mentors thus far in life. Susan is an ultra-accomplished public relations professional whose résumé and experience still wow me. The woman is a goddess, and she kindly shared with me one of her most enlightening professional moments.

Susan's first major position was with a prestigious city newspaper. She got along great with her boss, and after she had been working with him for about a year, he made a startling confession—he almost hadn't hired her. Why? you may ask. Was she competing against an avalanche of Harvard applicants? No. Did she have a criminal record? No. Was she just a dog to look at? Certainly not. It would appear that her boss had just broken off a romance of sorts with a woman named Susan when he began interviewing applicants to fill the position he did eventually give to my friend. He confessed he just didn't know if he could take having an office mate with the same name as his ex-honey.

The moral of this story, just in case you have lard in your head today, is that there are forces at work in corporate America that are beyond your control and, more important, beyond reason. Don't lose sleep if something comes out an unusual way. It could all just be thanks to the fact that you look like someone's deviant sister-in-law or weird southern cousin. Someone else's résumé paper had a prettier watermark, or . . . you get the idea. You must simply admit at the end of the day that there is a weird randomness in life. You are completely powerless next to it only if you always take things personally. Just run naked into the sunset and surrender; your sanity will be preserved.

Every group needs a leader.

Never be afraid to be alpha female when you know you're the woman for the job. However, humbly know you're not the woman for the job all the time.

I

t's only 11:00 A.M. and the day seems to be officially going to hell in a handbasket. Don't worry, it's merely time to step back and work up some positive mojo to take away the pain. The only way to survive the afternoon is to regroup with your senses and take a few minutes to gather your thoughts and prioritize. What *has* to be done by close of day—

set it directly in front of you. Whatever can wait—set it aside. Now remove all focus from the pile of papers on your desk and concentrate on your breathing instead. Take many deep breaths over the course of a few minutes, closing your eyes and just taking everything real slow. Will the five hundred photocopies you must have by five o'clock suddenly appear from the office fairy? No. But taking the time daily to earmark core tasks and calm your mental state ensures long-term professional Grooviness. Being wired, stressed, unorganized, unfocused— that just don't cut it. Stop, take control, get calm, confident, then going.

*In your job* there is a software program or general area of expertise that you simply don't have down well. The lack of knowledge regularly frustrates you, so it is time to eliminate the angst-causer once and for all. Lots of colleges and universities have night classes targeted toward working folks that could get you up to speed in whatever it is you may need help with. There are continuing education classes for everything from computer-related topics to management issues to how to build a better bookshelf. Bookstores offer row upon row of professional success texts and guides for your perusal. The point is weakness is only conquered by knowledge, so get off your haunches. When you can whiz through the creation of an Excel spreadsheet—if that's the thing you abhor doing now—you will have neutralized an element in your professional life that was draining your confidence and patience levels (in other words, you overpowered something that challenged Groove).

# Here's the game plan:

Make a list of all the job skills you wish to improve, then conquer them one at a time through classes or self-teaching. In time you will create for yourself a type of workplace nirvana. You can't control other people being block-heads or the copier machine going out yet again, but you can cultivate the psy-chological peace of feeling on top of your game by eradi-cating the shakier areas of your skill set.

Corporate America attempts to disconnect us from the living world from which we sprang with its sterile metal and concrete environment. It wants us to forget about carefree and reflective moments spent under trees, beside oceans, and actually just fresh air in general. It simply wants to have us slave away until we're sixty-four, then fire us before pension time. Don't buy into the static and artificial world of the office, seeing it as a *natural* habitat. It's all a construct designed to lull us into forgetting about the dynamic pulse of the beautiful world occurring outside the steel walls. As the office will never actively bring life our way (that would be too distracting), we must bring life to it to help keep us in tune with nature and our inner nymph. Keep some plants, flowers, or a terrarium in your office space—build a wild kingdom right there around your computer monitor. Eat your bagged lunch outside. Go out and feed birds and stray cats during breaks. Take a field trip to a park during lunch at least once a week. Get out of the box before you get all pasty white and die!

I t is time to start cutting down on coffee at the job. Why? Because it sucks the life out of you by fostering dependency and creating general antsy-ness. I know in our day of "let's all go to Starbucks and be cool drinking espresso" mentality this may seem old-fashioned advice, but I couldn't care less. Basically, you're injecting your body with a drug every morning to help you function and be alert, in other words, to just generally exist. We always cringe when we hear of someone who *has* to take sleeping pills to sleep and of those who *must* have alcohol after work to unwind—yet we hypocritically join the throng of zombie coworkers at the coffee station every morning for a hard-core caffeine hit ritual because that's *normal.* I love how we tell kids to "say no to drugs" and "drugs can't solve your problems," yet in the end we cling to the coffee tap, take Prozac, and suck on cigarettes (more on cancer sticks later) to help ourselves through the workday. The moral of this rant is that caffeine weakens us, poisons us, and thus steals Groove. Start decreasing your coffee intake until you can kiss the stuff good-bye. (Can I say tough love or what?)

**Y**ou dread going to your job every day. The alarm rings, and you have to peel yourself from under the covers. However, the boss is okay, you have decent coworkers and pay. What's wrong? Woman, you're in the wrong field and missing your true calling. Life is very short, and as we all know, we spend most of it at work. Start setting aside time for some self-reflection and research concerning other career paths that seriously intrigue you. Think about the things you adore doing for fun. Could they in any way be linked to a job you would look forward to going to in the morning? Talk to different people about what they do for a living. Do their positions sound interesting?

*S*et a goal to act on your new insights and research within the next year. Maybe you'll start off in a new field at the bottom rung of the ladder. Maybe you'll return to school for night classes that will prep you to switch vocations. Whatever you do, you've freed yourself to pursue your true dreams and interests. Sure, maybe you'll incur a tighter schedule and budget for a while, but eventually you will work yourself into an ultimately more fulfilling professional setting. Get to it.

**D**on't invest your entire identity in your job or job title; it's an aspect of your life, not its crux. If you sense you are beginning to completely tie your soul to your business card (or your friends just organized an intervention regarding the issue), it's time to cut back mentally. Start focusing on having more special time with your lover, friends, and hobbies in your after hours and weekends. It's simply time to inject more meaning and oomph into the other arenas of your life. Get on it pronto, mi amiga.

*D*o overtime only when it is *absolutely* necessary. In most all scenarios, salaried folk are paid for forty hours a week. If extensive overtime becomes a constant in your life, something needs to give. You need to negotiate for more vacation time, better technology, or an assistant, or perhaps just opt for another job. Our time is sacred. There are just more things to our lives than our desks, period. Be a good corporate clone and earn your paycheck by all means, but know where the line of exploitation begins and thus when your patience should end. Remember that extensive overtime actually devalues your paycheck and also negates the so-called free one to two weeks of vacation you're "given" in a year.

A tried but true confidence builder moves from the bedroom to the office place. Wear really sexy underwear not only on third dates but also to any dreaded presentation you must give.

Better to do a handful of projects well than a whole bunch in a half-a** fashion. Don't overextend yourself. Don't be afraid to say no when you have well enough to do already.

Try to get some exercise during the workday if at all possible. Some people are lucky and work right next to a gym, where they can instantly alleviate rage at office idiots during the lunch hour. If you're not that fortunate, you can at least take a lap or two around the building after you've eaten or during a break. Even a brief walk can lift your spirits and clear your mind before starting the second half of the day.

# Try to listen to music

during the workday as another means of injecting zest into your routine. Listening to music can help conquer the most evil or boring of tasks by putting spring in your step and giving you a rhythm to work along with. Unfortunately, there are some caveats. Number one: Happy music only. Sad ballads of lost love and virginity will certainly not inspire you to be productive or upbeat. Number two: If you're in the dead center of cube central, you can't very well blast tunes from your punk rock period on a normal CD player—opt for some inexpensive headphones instead. If you're fortunate enough to have your own little office hideaway, pat yourself on the back (and bite me!). Close your door when you're in the true midst of terrible work and really let the music play. We certainly need to be accessible to people who need us, that's part of a job. However, very rarely are things in such a state that

you have to be *immediately* available to any and everyone who desires to interrupt you. People can leave
voice mails and E-mails that you can quickly address
after you wrap up music-filled work marathons. If any-
body is a humbug about it, tell her that taking care of
one's self at work is not just for divas anymore. Now
go stock up at the music store.

Straighten up your damn posture, you're killing your back hunching over that desk. You'll feel and appear more confident, thus fooling office rats into thinking you are far too on top of things to be trifled with.

Major stress at work sometimes stems from things we simply can't control. Someone screwed you over by not helping out, the server and printers just went down *again*. You want to scream but can't, due to HR's hyper-strict noise violation policies. What you can do is sing a special song a coworker once so generously shared with me. Stand up at your desk and just sing this soft little tune to yourself.

*Push out the jiiiive . . .*
(extend your arms and palms out)

*Bring in the loooove . . .*
(bring arms and palms back toward chest)

*One more time . . .*
*Push out the jiiiive . . .*
*Bring in the loooove . . .*

Sing this little ditty to your beloved colleagues when they too are stressed. They think you're nuts anyway now because of that terrarium you've built.

*B*e sure you have several great photos around of your family, pets, and friends. Sadly enough, we see more of our coworkers than we do of them, and we need a little something there to remind us of what is waiting for us in our off-hours. Besides, by hanging photos in your work space you'll appear sensitive, and people will start thinking you can't be that much of a wench if you own a really cute dog that you proudly display all over the place.

*I*f your place of work has an intramural league or some type of casual sports team designed for kicks, join it. Forget Outward Bound trust courses! The best way to bond with your coworkers is by laughing at their lack of hand-eye coordination on a volleyball court. (And they of course will laugh at you, so come prepared.) If no program currently exists, get some brownie points from everyone by starting one.

Strive to cultivate a general sense of calm and peace at work. We can control our existence in our home life, but the office as a rule contains all types of chaos and mayhem. We can't control or foresee all the havoc a client or project may create, but we are very much in control of the Groove we will let ourselves lose while handling the inevitable screwups, delays, mishaps, and miscommunications that plague professional life. Mark your stress boundaries and know when you're about to reach them, then stop hanging on so damn tight. And leave it all at the door on your way home at night.

Getting Groove Back in Your

# Relationships

It is the friends
you can call up at 4:00 A.M.
that matter.

—*Marlene Dietrich*

S ave the money you set aside for the obligatory birthday gift for the *friend* with whom you are no longer close. Spend it on yourself instead. Go buy a decadent box of chocolate-dipped strawberries from those fine Godiva folks and scarf them under a tree, celebrating your ability to sever the old and seek out the new. That relationship had a place in your past, and guess what, we call it the *past* for a reason—move on. Besides, the hussy never returned that favorite belt of yours she borrowed; hence, it's time to trot toward evolution.

Certainly don't be a doormat, but do what you can to always be of help to your friends. It simply makes you feel great. Cook dinner for the girlfriend who has slaved away doing late nights at work or treat her to a manicure. Help a friend or coworker move, because moving just plain bites. You get the idea. Helping others relieves stress, builds closeness, and plain can't hurt anything (unless you're put in charge of dusting china while intoxicated). In the same vein, general community service is another excellent means to get Groove back. Getting out in the world and helping and meeting new people is all worthwhile and feel-good. Remember you're just another person though, not love-me-I'm-Joan-of-Arc. I can't stand those people who I know really do volunteer work just so they can advertise how sensitive and special they are. Bleecchhh! Damn all those broads.

I f you really don't like your current romantic interest, if he really doesn't make you happy, *dump him.* Life is short, don't waste your time.

43

The most self-defeating thing you can do in your life is be dishonest in your relationships with others. The farce of maintaining a happy face completely zaps your energy, and a lifetime of such charades will simply transform you into a tired and blasé personage. Don't be a hussy to yourself in this most important regard.

It's true: Never loan a friend money. Money can have this creepy property of corrupting relationships it enters. Just the fact that it's one of the leading causes of divorce is more than testament to that. Don't learn this one the hard way, just trust me, O young grasshopper who comes seeking wisdom.

# Get rid of everything in your home that came from old boyfriends or ex-husbands

who turned out to be whoremongers, stalkers, and/or couch potatoes. That stuff is unconsciously making you think about people who sucked the life out of you. If it's cheap stuff, give it to Goodwill or some other charity. If it is rich stuff, sell it or give it to a good friend who has always had eyes for it. Anyway, get all the bad stuff out of your space so you can get your Groove back.

I give this harsh-sounding advice out of genuine concern for women and children. Don't have kids if you know you really don't want to parent. Don't do it just because it's still very much expected of women. Don't have a child for what it could do for you at all, but for what you could make possible for a child in this crazy world. Do it because you approach motherhood with a pure and selfless heart, and feel very informed about the sacrifice you are making in regard to your personal time and space.

Bringing another person onto the planet is a *huge deal*. You're completely responsible for a helpless person's emotional, physical, and social development—and all entailing financial needs. You're not a bad person if you know you just can't take this plunge. Bad people breed like rabbits and basically just have kids around to serve as suburban decor. We've all seen them, those parents who seem about as interested in their offsprings' healthy development as an Olympic athlete with a silver medal (God, I never liked Nancy Kerrigan). Those people leave my stomach ill. Please don't be them, they're a selfish and evil force. Lead a childless life if that is what your heart dictates as best, and happily know you're not dragging down any innocent third parties in your daily routine.

**P**erhaps you already have some kids, and though it's hectic at times, you feel very fulfilled in the parental role, are learning from your mistakes, and are always trying to be the best parent you can. That is absolutely wonderful. Congratulate yourself for being so mature and focused on establishing a healthy home. Keep moving forward with your winning formula.

Perhaps you have kids, and honestly, you're just not feeling great about motherhood. It's time for you to do some soul-searching and seek counseling immediately. This is an issue that will fester in your soul until you reach some resolution and perspective. I'm not recommending counseling because you're "abnormal" but because counselors are confidential sounding boards who can guide you to some insight and solutions for your pain. Friends and family can be very unsympathetic toward the feelings you're experiencing because as a culture we still support the myth that women find total and "natural" fulfillment through bearing fruit. Admitting you don't feel real fulfilled challenges a cornerstone of our patriarchy and gets some folks antsy, and thus not too supportive. You're not a freak at all, but one fact remains: You brought some people into the world who depend on you. Most likely they are sensing your frustration because kids aren't stupid. Get some help, yesterday, for their sake as well as your own.

You know the scene—you're in a terrible fight about topic X with a friend or lover. Mean verbal assaults are flying right and left, and all of a sudden the words spewing out of your mouth no longer have anything to do with the proper place to put folded washrags or whose turn it is to clean the toilet. Instead, the words are suddenly more along the lines of "you never want to have sex anymore and I can't stand it" or "you have never accepted me for what I really am." Alas, these harsh gems proclaim the true issues troubling the relationship. Don't ignore these bitter outbursts, no matter how much you or the other party may want to dismiss them as mere "I was just trying to hurt you" isms. It's hard work to address the rough content of our more passionate and honest declarations, but be certain all will turn even uglier if these monsters are left to grow larger.

Here's another area to add to your spring-cleaning list. Every now and then you find yourself with a couple of acquaintances who are really only concerned with not missing weekly manicure appointments. Slough off those vixens like dead skin cells. Rub them right off and keep moving in the direction of your Groove. Seek out people from whom you can learn and whom you honestly admire and wish to emulate.

top and think about those relationships you maintain out of duty. Stop acting like you're a happy daughter/sister/cousin/granddaughter if these relationships do not truly bring you joy. Our loved ones are as imperfect as we and are thus allowed a few quirks, but there are boundaries as to what we should have to endure over the course of our lives. Stop being such a friggin' Girl Scout.

Make a point to befriend your neighbors, cultivating a kindly relationship with them. We all know the drill, we used to have communities in America. Then we all started working our rears off and moving far away from our roots to big cities to get richer and be cosmopolitan. The result is a lonely life sometimes for ourselves and our neighbors, who are in the same boat with us. We must help foster a sense of community to fight feelings of isolation. If you have leftovers from dinner and the couple next door is fighting the flu, take some meat loaf to them—don't fear contagion. Mow their lawn if they had to flee town to be with a sick relative. Fuss over their outdoor pets. One day when the world is not treating you right, a friendly neighbor will be there to return the favor.

# Start taking more photographs

of friends, family, trips, and daily life. It may seem nutty, but I secretly think we sometimes feel we lead lackluster lives because we never really open our eyes to how much *is* actually happening around us. Pets are doing funny poses by the fireplace; friends are having us over or coming to see us; we're having a Halloween dress-up day at the office, et cetera. We have a tendency to let all this blur together.

## Solution:

Excessive documentation. Keep your camera loaded and batteries charged in a central place in the home. Take that picture of Rover looking cute on the couch with your honey. Take the camera to the casual dinner party friends are hosting and snap away. Take it to work when there is a special office function. Start a photo album or scrapbook you can look at when your existence is feeling uneventful. You'll realize you're surrounded by many fun and crazy goings-on. Also, giving away double prints of photos to friends and family makes them feel Groovy, too. It gives them material for their own photo albums, and the "trouble" you take to do this simple act makes them feel special. C'mon now, take pictures, spread the love, and invest in Kodak to offset your new level of film expenditure.

*L*ive without secrets from the person who has stolen your heart. I don't mean those tiny ones, like how you detest the way he fanatically folds bath towels—we're talking deathbed quality only here. Secrets take too much energy to hide over a lifetime, and they just ain't worth it.

There is a best friend who may be in a city far away who you love and who has always loved you unconditionally and supported you and soothed you in a way no one else can even understand. Save up for a plane ticket. You need to see her in person as often as possible.

59

If festivities such as Christmas, Hanukkah, Sunday dinners, or other family occasions do nothing but fill you with dread and discomfort, wake up! You are a human being with free will—you don't have to attend. This simple thought may at first strike you as too shocking to even consider.

Get over it and have a fun holiday celebration that's on your own terms.

Buy ten pink flamingos and hide them in the garage or car trunk. Every now and then, sneak one onto the lawn of a neighbor or friend you really like. Maybe do it on a day when life isn't treating them so well. They will be humored and perplexed, and you will get a rush from the fun deviousness of the exercise. Eventually you will confess or be caught. Either way, this is just another trick for creating fun and zaniness for yourself and others.

Patronize female-owned businesses and opt to have female professionals (such as doctors or saleswomen) service you in lieu of their male colleagues. It's taken *years* for it to be "okay" to be a working woman in America, though we still get flak from relatives, certain conservative groups, and the media. We all know someone who has been sexually harassed at work, the glass ceiling routine, and the ongoing gender-based pay gap that exists across the nation in all industries. Long story short, we need to support one another in the realm of business. The power to upset the obstacles still set before us may well lie in how we wield our very own checkbooks.

Get in touch with the people
who you feel have shown you
the greatest kindness or enriched
your life the most. Thank
them. Enough said. If it has to
be at a gravestone, so be it. They
will hear you. It's really
important we take the time to
realize what others have added
to our lives and acknowledge it.
It helps us see ourselves in
an entirely new way.

Know that not *every* argument in a relationship warrants a six-hour postfight analysis and forgiveness segment. Some days we're simply cranky and out of spirits and our partners are the same way. When there is a fight about a damn stupid thing, let it go. Go for some back rubbing instead. Save the intense mental energy for whenever you decide to take that darn GRE.

*I*n your quest to improve personal Groove levels, you must be careful not to undermine the Groove of others. Don't be intentionally cruel or catty to anyone. Groove will *not* coexist with bitchiness; it will instead wither away in its presence. The only exceptions to this rule are the following:

*1.* You can be a wench to those trust-fund types who are much deserving of some slapping around by trash such as yourself.

*2.* You can defend an innocent person some rat is victimizing (this innocent person may sometimes be yourself).

Besides these two scenarios, try to cut down on your road rage and general snippiness with others. In the end, ye shall reap more Groove, baby.

You know those people you dread to see on your caller ID—they don't own your soul. Pick up the phone and tell them however you really feel about the relationship. I don't care who it is—mother, priest, or telemarketer. It's hard the first time—you'll feel like you're doing *Abs of Steel,* but it has to be done. Only then can the other people know what they can do to fix or improve the relationship, and that there is actually a problem. You may have the sad realization that they are selfish rats who don't desire to really improve anything. Leave them to their own sorry selves and move on with your life. Also, there are sadly people in our lives who cannot comprehend our feelings and try to pretend that everything is all right. We can't reach those who don't want to be reached. Be content that you have gotten your sentiments off your chest, and that you have found the limits of your relations with them. Then let it go.

# Getting Groove Back in Your

# Soul

We are the hero of
our own story.

—Mary McCarthy

top beating yourself up because you're not what you said you'd become when you were a little girl. Okay, so you didn't get an Olympic gold medal or become an ambassador to the UN. It's true our lives don't always deal us the cards we need to get the grandiose life, but get real, you're a born couch potato and you detest politics. Why should you feel guilty any longer for not doing something that doesn't fit your personality anyway? There's nothing wrong with *not* being a famous athlete or political figure. There's lots of us out here, and we're okay people. Join us. Love us. Become one with us.

Get some
new white socks.

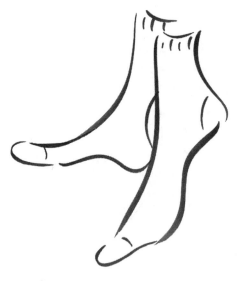

They feel so fine.

It's easier to sit on our rear ends while the rest of the world runs past us, complaining occasionally that we are kind of bored with life. It takes energy to stand up and make a point to stay in touch with a friend or budget for the trip we always say we want to take. If you want to just keep sitting on your porch, that's fine. But don't be surprised when we call you a very boring and very predictable old fart who is about as complex as an amoeba.

reat yourself to fresh flowers on a fairly regular basis. I mean, if you're just waiting for the men in your life to get them for you those one or two days a year, that's pretty sad. Flowers instantly uplift your mood, and there is nothing truly as beautiful to behold in nature. You can get some at the grocery store these days for just a few dollars, so stock up, even if it's only a daisy or two a week.

ecome a connoisseur of the bubble bath. I personally think that baths relax me so much because they're as close as I can get to that safe feeling of being in the womb—with all the gross, warm fluid protecting me. I guess that's getting too confessional, though. Suffice it to say that it's a proven fact hot baths are relaxing. Make it a habit at least four times a week to escape to the bathtub with Calgon or whatever else can take you away. Don't feel guilty about buying really good bath products either; you can try to deduct them at tax time as a medical expense (if you have a shady accountant).

*Nudity is a lost art.*
Practice it. Your skin is your own, and
you should really grow to appreciate
your body and be comfortable in it.
Every one of your curves is uniquely yours,
your signature version of the lovely female
form. Revel in your nature-given attractiveness.
Don't go to a freaky nudist colony; those places
are probably just fronts for antigovernment
groups anyway. But while in your home, make
yourself *at home* by loading the dishwasher
and reading the classics buck naked. Your
lover(s) will be forever enamored of your quirki-
ness (and accessibility), and you'll begin to really
love and appreciate every "flaw" you perceive
you have because extensive nudity destroys
feelings of self-consciousness and shame. Hey,
I'm topless as I write this, and look how
inspired my writing is (no kidding! Mom will be
so proud!).

Guiltlessly cultivate your shoe-buying fetish. Go for green ones, red ones, sparkly ones, with straps or without, dressy, casual, whatever you want. Treat your feet well, though, staying clear of extreme high heels.

*G*ive up your cooking obsession because I'm over it. I'm tired of hearing female acquaintances gripe about how much time they have to spend in the kitchen—time that was truly unfulfilling and that may as well have been an aerobics session from hell in terms of enjoyment. Invest in some twenty-minute-or-less recipe books, spend ten minutes doing a basic menu plan for the week, and go to the grocery store *once* weekly for whatever it is you may need.

*O*nly one thing is certain in this world, and that is that we're going to die someday. Let me translate this for you. It means we have a limited number of minutes to fill with joy and contentment on this planet. Hmmm . . . do I want to spend time lounging with my pets, plants, and honey, or shall I get all anxious trying to fix another botched and burned attempt at that chicken Parmesan recipe I copied off the HGTV Web site? You get the idea. There are just some sucky activities that have to be performed before the day is done, but the trick is to shave as much time and worry from their duration as possible.

*f* you like cooking, that's great. Keep creating those scones from scratch and six-course meals that culminate with a serving of smoked salmon you had specially sent from Alaska. The rest of us will pitch in and get you a crown to wear since you're obviously so perfect. Just don't be surprised when you learn jokes about your fanatical lifestyle are the best ones from poker night. Pass me some peanut butter, girlfriend!

Buy a feather boa at a costume shop or Halloween clearance sale. Get in the habit of tossing it on when you're doing fun or relaxing activities at home. For instance, you could wear your boa as you read your trashy romance novels at night. (Don't lie, I know all women have secretly read at least a couple of these sex-me-now-and-like-it yarns for a jolly.)

o on a TV diet. Allow yourself to watch only three or four shallow sitcoms and a couple of movies a week. TV really eats into our time, and sadly, it really doesn't do that much for us in return. It just plain puts trash in our heads. (The only exception would be if you watch a lot of really stimulating programs, such as documentaries featuring baboon-mating practices, and feel such programming really increases your appreciation of the world.) Same with surfing the Internet. Staying up till 3:00 A.M. to download animated cartoons or sit in on goofy chat rooms isn't critical to our existence, so set a strict limit on how much time you'll allow for such mind-numbing experiences.

$\int$ tart drinking water like you're leaving for the Sahara tomorrow. It flushes out our systems like nothing else can and cleanses us. You can't beat that with a stick.

G o to a local museum and peruse the gallery of art which you usually hate and which provides you no inspiration or insight. (For me, this was the modernist section for a long period.) Select several art pieces there and spend ten to fifteen minutes *really* studying each one. Honestly try to figure out what in the world is going on with them (perhaps contemplating what drug the painter/sculptor might have been abusing). Look at every line, shade, color, object, hint of movement, drama, everything. Consider the highbrow analysis the museum provides as well. Maybe do more research after-ward on a work that really confuses you or (big gulp) becomes suddenly aesthetically appealing. The point of all this (and there is one) is to reopen your mind to different visions and perspectives of the world by venturing outside that comfy little box you've created for yourself mentally.

When we're young, we're all for expanding our worldview and being deep thinking and philosophical, for considering new and different things. As we age, though, we simply tend to get a bit rusty because of routine. Studying art can be a wonderful vehicle for getting back in the saddle intellectually. So get out there, your brain cells are in dire straits.

## Note:

A fun variation on this exercise is to substitute music for artwork. Yet another adaptation would be to read the biography or literature of a person whose lifestyle/personal politics you currently judge to be "abnormal." The goal is just to expose yourself to anything that could really stimulate your gray matter.

If you spend more than fifteen minutes in the morning on your face and hair, get over yourself. Start to consider the idea that maybe, just maybe, you don't need lots of war paint and hairspray to be a good-looking hot momma. Open yourself to the notion that you are damn well good enough as you are, that you're a striking person unadorned. Little by little, wean yourself from complex cosmetics and haircuts. Have faith in a more natural look, my dear, because it's attitude and Groove that attract love and admiration from a soul mate, not neurotic dedication to intensive cosmetic regimens.

To help get yourself started, sit down and make a list of all the things you can do with the time and money you now dedicate to personal grooming. You could sleep in longer in the morning with your honey (hey, there's a great chance this could lead to more sex, too—double score!). You could apply the saved money toward upgrading next year's vacation. Do this, do that, do whatever—just remember to fill your time with fun, not unnecessary and costly maintenance work.

Make peace with your childhood roots. Know you're the unique person you are today because of the licks you took as a youngster and the particular environment you survived. Maybe you need some help from a counselor on this one, and that's fine. Maybe you need to give certain people a piece of your mind, and that's fine, too. Do *whatever* you need to do to eliminate any pain you still might have once and for all. When you're finally done, though, celebrate. I like margaritas myself, but I don't know what your poison is.

There is some neat event or place in your town that everyone raves about which you have never bothered to visit. You have always somehow avoided it or missed it. Go and have a good time and be done with it. And wear a hat.

*Give up all housework
for two to three weeks.*

Be horrified when you realize how much of your life has been unnecessarily sucked out of you while you were pushing around a Hoover. Your house or apartment really won't look that bad, but clean it anyway and then let it go for another two or three weeks. Repeat this process over and over again. This exercise will numb you to that notion that everything in a woman's home must be spotless and puritanically sanitized every other day. There will always be dust bunnies in the limited days of our lives. However, there are many enriching experiences and passions which we need to make time for, and which are far better for improving Groove. Never pass up anything that could be fun because you feel you should wash or clean some stupid thing. In the grand scheme of life, being known for keeping a tidy house is really not worth the cost.

Stop eating out at the same restaurants and eating the same dishes. Get some spice in your life. Seek out new eating establishments and intentionally try new types of foods and drinks. Stop going with just the same old same old—give your palate an adventure. Drag your lover and friends along as well so they can do the same.

**Q**uit smoking. Must I insult your intelligence by elaborating? I have both friends and relatives who would cross the Andes naked with mountain gorillas serving as trail guides in order to take one puff of a cigarette. Despite the mounting effects on their day-to-day health, they just don't give a damn. They don't care about yellow teeth, dragon breath, wrinkly mouths, cancer, shortness of breath, or the growing concerns of their friends and family.

If you smoke, you are exposing your body to an addictive substance that literally shortens life and lessens its quality. In addition, your secondhand smoke attacks other people's health, you're polluting the planet, and you're lining the pockets of heartless companies who for decades have denied the negative effects of their products. Stand up for yourself once and for all and lay the mothers down. You'll be stronger for it, and your body will love you again after all the nastiness is flushed from your system—what a way to get some Groove back.

On a side note, I have for years had to laugh at the terrible hypocrisy exhibited by parents who smoke. "Young Megan and Bob Jr., take your vitamins, eat your vegetables, wash your hands, and go to the doctor and dentist without a fuss so you can grow up healthy and strong. Now has either of you seen my cancer sticks? I've gotta have one right now or I'm gonna die."

*I*n our day of one-hour dry cleaning and film development/FedEx for next morning delivery/supersize my fries now and hurry 'cause I must return to work from this drive-through/page me and call me on my cell phone to reach me any time/fight rush hour/save the planet pronto culture, it's really hard to just sit still and relax our minds and bodies. Start at least thinking about thinking about pursuing meditation. I advise this humbly as the practice is still sometimes associated with crystal-sucking, tree-hugging fanatics. However, despite any bad press, it's been a tried and true ritual for centuries of people looking to center and calm themselves. Personally, I'm so hyper and wired I've yet to achieve blissful all-knowingness and peace through meditation. But I figure, hell, the best part of a road trip is usually the drive there, so I'm just doing the best I can and enjoying the mental exercise. In all seriousness, please consider learning more about this sacred practice. Even if you never completely rival some bald dude's inner serenity, you'll certainly still be ahead of those who never even gave it a shot.

Dig out all the pretty things you usually save for when company comes over or for the holidays. Whatever it is, get it out and use it. I'll warn you right now, a piece of china or crystal will eventually get broken as a result of increased use, but that's okay. It's stupid to condemn nice things we own to a life of Styrofoam-wrapped seclusion when we could enjoy them and spoil ourselves a bit with their constant presence. Pamper yourself and don't waste nice towels, tablecloths, and whatever else any longer. It only makes good sense.

*R*ead more. Keep a good book at your side at all times. Make it a goal to finish at least two books a month. Reading is wonderful and relaxing brain food, and it mentally keeps us on our toes.

I hate to bring this up because we all initially cringe at the idea, but you really do need to exercise and get into shape. Now don't freak out on me. I know I've been wooing you with all these fun things to do and think about, and now you feel betrayed since I've let the terrible *E* word inside our inner sanctum. Well, stop being a big baby. Exercise is critical to getting your Groove back because it offers instant stress relief and an opportunity to mentally zone out and review your thoughts as you tread along doing whatever. There aren't too many outlets that can provide these wonderful things for us so immediately, and throw in the added kudos of improved health and self-image. You don't need to spend big money at a gym, you don't need a fancy Nike wardrobe. Just make some time to take a daily thirty-minute walk and see how much you come to enjoy and relish its rejuvenating powers. Maybe eventually you'll move on to more advanced exercise, and that's great. Maybe you'll just stick with the walking, and that's great, too. Just get off the couch and reap the Groovy benefits exercise can offer.

I'll never understand it. We go to doctors and read medical texts to learn how to stay healthy. We turn to cookbooks and cooking shows to outline exact recipes and cooking techniques. We read self-help books out the yin-yang to learn how to soothe our inner children. We go to therapists to find out how to deal with our relatives. We'll look into anything that might improve our sex lives. We hire personal trainers to get us in shape. We reference *The Old Farmer's Almanac* when picking a date for the annual family picnic. We attend golf clinics to achieve a better swing. We consult with local nurserymen about how to grow a better rosebush. We utilize all types of resources for all sorts of things, yet most people leave their financial future and well-being to chance. Lots of us do crappy jobs of budgeting, think retirement is too far away to even worry about, make major purchases without research or thought of financial implications, and generally live beyond our means by charging away with credit cards.

The psychological cost of living with too much debt and in general financial chaos is very high. Seek out the services of a certified financial adviser or planner. (Do a little research at the bookstore to determine which will be best for you. You don't want to consult with anyone just because she or he sports some fancy-sounding titles, or someone who is working on commission, because her or his advice might be biased.) These folks analyze their clients' income, debts, and financial goals in order to create sound budgets that lead to good saving and spending habits. Feeling secure means feeling Groovy, so take the steps now that will allow for harmonious financial standing in the present and in the future.

**B**uy some leather pants and just walk around in them one day. The neighbors won't know what in the hell to think as you're cackling in your new duds while doing some make-believe weeding. (Or better yet, save them for the neighborhood block party!) The soccer moms in the grocery aisles will shield their impressionable young children from you—you mysterious leather-pants-wearing woman.

Travel to Texas once in your life and watch the sun set. After visiting fifteen countries, I have to say a Texas sunset is the prettiest and most uplifting I've ever seen. Besides, all that "don't mess with Texas" attitude is a sight to see—those people are a mess. Try to go during bluebonnet season, too.

# Dance!!!!!!

Do the electric slide in your jammies in the living room. Grab all the girls for a night out at a swinging place. Tango in the driveway. Just dance! Dancing is a universal venue for fun and letting your hair down. And hair being down is directly proportionate to Groove being up. I'm particularly proud I've been the dancing fool at all wedding receptions I've attended in recent years. My friends think I'm a loon, but I've just wanted to make sure that all those DJs and bands were earning their money. Long live the conga line!

# Woohoo!

Bimonthly manicures never killed anyone.

A manicurist's pampering and massaging

makes you feel like a queen,

and what's wrong with that?

Do a makeover on your magazine reading list. Once and for all, *stop* reading those trashy beauty magazines! Everyone and her sister knows by now that the women depicted are all air-brushed to perfection, and that the editorial content of "articles" is determined for the most part by whatever gives good lip service to advertisers. The advertisers pay *big bucks* to throw in ads that are designed to make us feel unglamorous and physically

lacking so we'll feel compelled to buy their products, which conveniently promise to cure our terrible disfigurements and poor wardrobes. Our lives aren't pathetic because we're not romping through meadows in coifed 'dos and perfumed brassieres with sexy male models. Au contraire, mon frère. Our lives are pathetic only if we keep paying three to five dollars a hit for literature that's infested with crappy lies we take for truth. Stop the madness! Buy magazines that tickle your intellect and sense of humor, not ones that drain your self-esteem and wallet.

Go to the garage, attic, or barn and dig up that box that has all your cool childhood and teenage music. You may have trouble playing the records, but throw those tapes and CDs in and enjoy making fun of yourself and the evolution of your taste. Think about how much you have grown and matured as a person, and pat yourself on the back for all the phases you've survived. Stop and think about why you favored certain music or musicians at different points in time. Music preference can be a great indicator of emotional states and health. See if this perspective gives you any new insights into your present or past self. Get Freudian, woman!

*I*n your home or apartment, you need a special nook just for you. Virginia Woolf was right about a woman needing a room of her own, but in the modern world we may have to improvise a bit. Perhaps your special haven could be a reading chair in a corner, or a little

108

place on the deck where you can look at your garden. Wherever it may be, give it your signature—make it *your* pad. Decorate it just the way you like, in a way that really soothes you. Go there and just *be* for at least a few minutes every day so you can reflect on the day's experiences. Read stimulating books there. Doodle. Paint. Write a real letter to a real friend. Organize your photo album. Write in a journal. The only rule is not to do *anything* negative in this space. Always treat it as a safe zone. Don't hold arguments there, or make phone calls. Leave it only when you're ready to, not just because the phone is ringing or a load of laundry needs to be done. Things like that can wait. When you know you do need to get back to routine, acknowledge that, but take a few deep breaths and *then* leave your special place.

After creating your special place, you actually need to revisit the way you've decorated your entire home. As a matter a fact, you need to take a good long walk around the house and see if you still even like what's around you. I'm not saying you need to watch *This Old House* for the next five months straight, but it's time to pep up your home and really transform it into a beautiful and relaxing environment. Call a charity to come and get all the stuff you don't find appealing anymore and then leisurely begin a room-by-room overhaul. You don't need to give away your firstborn to achieve a home you're proud to call your own.

Just throw up some new paint and scour yard sales and outlet stores for new furnishings and decor items. You can get a lot of bang for your buck by shopping smart and learning how to do some simple handiwork on your own. Every now and then, though, treat yourself to an item that just grabs you, be it exquisite bedroom curtains or a piece of artwork. Redecorating is a creative, fun, and engaging process, and the finished result will be a home you'll feel is charged with Grooviness.

Dress up in a persona that is not what people would generally call *you* at all. You could simulate sloppiness, suburban housewifeness, Hooker Barbieness (the look of any modern Barbie), or perhaps a beatnik poet look. In the "disguise," go to the grocery store, the post office, the mall, a party, wherever. The goal is not to make you think you're actually another person but just to allow you the chance to dwell on the way you usually present yourself to the world and why you do it. Why is the raised eyebrow your trampy Barbie miniskirt just elicited bothering you? Why do you usually hide your body? Are you ashamed of it?

If so, why? And what would it take to change that self-image? Why do you feel uncomfortable in an outfit that isn't expensive looking? Why does a thirty-dollar outfit make you feel you must appear destitute? You've received tons of compliments today on the pastel green pantsuit you dressed up in, so why *do* you always wear black? Do you secretly fear trying to figure out color coordination? Are you in mourning for something you weren't aware of? Get to know the persona you've created for yourself via your choice of wardrobe. This is the only way to realize you may well be ready for a change.

Pursue your passions,
never let them go by the wayside.

# Conclusion

To keep a lamp burning
we have to keep putting oil
to it.

*—Mother Teresa*

Well, so you're done with the book. You're pumped, you're charged, you've already purchased a black feather boa, and that's wonderful. Doing just one thing in this book is all you need to start getting your Groove back.

Before beginning though, one critical point must be addressed. Keeping high Groove levels isn't rocket science, but it is an ongoing enterprise. It's like staying fit and trim. If you don't pay attention to exercise and healthy eating on a daily basis, you simply don't achieve and maintain top form.

The stress and hubbub of everyday life will never end its incessant assault on our senses; that's a simple fact. So to counter this malevolence, we must be constantly committed to making sure we're taking care of ourselves. If we slack off in this effort for even just a minute, we make way for tension and negativity to overtake our spunk, our zest, our unadulterated joy with life—our Groove. Make a commitment to yourself never to let this happen again. Do the exercises in this book gradually over time, and explore any other activities they may lead you to. Always be on the lookout for scenarios, relationships, or environments that are bound to suck the life out of ya and steer clear.

Now let your hair down, crack the whip, and go for the Groove.